THE WARMTH AND WONDER OF

Christmas

THE WARMTH AND WONDER OF

Christmas

Devotions to Put a Glow in the Heart of a Family

by

ROBERT STRAND

New Leaf Press

First printing: July 1996
Second printing: October 1996

ISBN: 0-89221-335-3
Library of Congress Number: 96-69690

The Original Christmas Story

ABOUT THAT TIME CAESAR AUGUSTUS ordered a census to be taken throughout the Empire. This was the first census when Quirinius was governor of Syria. Everyone had to travel to his own ancestral hometown to be accounted for. So Joseph went from the Galilean town of Nazareth up to Bethlehem in Judea, David's town, for the census. As a descendent of David, he had to go there. He went with Mary, his fiancee, who was pregnant.

WHILE THEY WERE THERE, the time came for her to give birth. She gave birth to a son, her firstborn. She wrapped him in a blanket and laid him in a manger, because there was no room in the hostel.

THERE WERE SHEEPHERDERS camping in the neighborhood. They had set nightwatches over their sheep. Suddenly, God's angel stood among them and God's glory blazed around them. They were terrified. The angel said, "Don't be afraid. I'm here to announce a great and joyful event that is meant for everybody, worldwide: **A Saviour has just been born in David's town, a Saviour who is Messiah and Master.** This is what you're to look for: a baby wrapped in a blanket and lying in a manger."

AT ONCE THE ANGEL was joined by a huge angelic choir singing God's praises:

> *"GLORY TO GOD IN THE HEAVENLY HEIGHTS,*
> *PEACE TO ALL MEN AND WOMEN*
> *ON EARTH WHO PLEASE HIM."*

AS THE ANGEL CHOIR withdrew into heaven, the sheepherders talked it over. "Let's get over to Bethlehem as fast as we can and see for ourselves what God has revealed to us." They left running and found Mary and Joseph, and the baby lying in the manger. Seeing was believing . . . they told everyone they met what the angels had said about this child. Everyone who heard the sheepherders was likewise impressed.

MARY KEPT ALL THESE THINGS TO HERSELF, holding them dear, deep within herself. The sheepherders returned and let loose, glorifying and praising God for everything they had heard and seen. It turned out exactly the way they'd been told!

Luke 2:1-20 from *The Message*, Eugene Peterson, translator, (Colorado Springs, CO: NavPress).

The Innkeeper

I only did what you have done
A thousand times or more
When Joseph came to Bethlehem
And knocked upon my door

I did not turn the Christ away
With alibi so deft.
Like you, I simply gave to Him
Whatever I had left.

(B. P. Baker)

The Night of Wonder

I grew up believing that Christmas was a time when strange and wonderful things happened, when wise and royal visitors came riding, when barnyard animals talked at midnight, and . . . in the light of a fabulous star . . . God came down to us as a little child. For me, Christmas has always been a time of enchantment, but never more so than the year my youngest, Marty, was eight.

That was the year my children and I moved into a cozy trailer in a forested area just outside of Redmond, Washington. Even the winter rains that swept down Puget Sound to douse our home could not dampen our spirits as the holiday approached.

Throughout that December, Marty had been the busiest and most spirited of us all. He was a cheerful, blond-haired boy who cocked his head like a puppy when you talked to him. He was deaf in his left ear. But he never complained about his condition.

For weeks I had been watching him, noticing that something was going on that he was not telling me about. I saw how eagerly he made his bed and took out the trash, how carefully he set the table and helped Rick and Pam prepare dinner before I got home from work. I saw how he silently collected his tiny allowance and tucked it away, spending not a cent of it. I had no idea what all this quiet activity was about, but I suspected it had something to do with Kenny.

Kenny was Marty's best friend, and ever since they had found each other in the springtime, they were inseparable. Their world was the meadow, a horse pasture broken by a small winding stream, where they would catch frogs and snakes, search for arrowheads or hidden treasure, or feed peanuts to the squirrels.

Times were hard for our little family, and we had to scrimp to get by. But with my job as a meat wrapper and a lot of ingenuity, we managed to have elegance on a shoestring.

But not Kenny's family. They were desperately poor, and his mother struggled to feed and clothe her two children. They were a good, solid family, but Kenny's mom was very proud, and she had strict rules.

How we worked, as we did each year, to make our home festive for the holidays! Ours was a handcrafted Christmas of gifts hidden away and ornaments strung about the place.

Marty and Kenny would sometimes sit still at the table long enough to help make cornucopias or weave little baskets for the tree. But then one would whisper to the other, and they would be out the door and sliding cautiously under the electric fence into the horse pasture that separated our home from Kenny's.

One night, shortly before Christmas, when my hands were

deep in cookie dough, Marty came to me, and in a tone mixed with pleasure and pride, he said, "Mom, I've bought Kenny a Christmas present. Want to see it? It's something he's wanted for a long time."

After carefully wiping his hands on a dish towel, he pulled from his pocket a small box. Lifting the lid, I gazed at the instrument my son had been saving all those allowances to buy . . . a little compass to point an eight-year-old adventurer through the woods.

"It's a lovely gift, Martin," I said, but even as I spoke, a disturbing thought came to mind. I knew how Kenny's mother felt about their poverty. They could barely afford to exchange gifts among themselves. Giving presents to others was out of the question. I was sure that Kenny's proud mother would not permit her son to receive something he could not return in kind.

Gently, carefully, I talked over the problem with Marty. He understood what I was saying.

"I know, Mom, I know! But what if it was a secret? What if they never found out who gave it?"

I didn't know how to answer him. I just didn't know.

The day before Christmas dawned rainy, cold, and gray.

The three kids and I put the finishing touches on Christmas secrets and prepared for family and friends who would be dropping by.

Night settled in. The rain continued. I looked out the window over the sink and felt an odd sadness. How mundane the rain seemed for a Christmas Eve! Would wise and royal men come riding on such a night? I doubted it. It seemed to me that strange and wonderful things happened only on clear nights when one could at least see a star in the heavens.

I turned away from the window, and as I checked on the ham warming in the oven, I saw Marty slip out the door. He wore his coat over his pajamas and clutched a tiny, colorfully wrapped box.

Down through the soggy pasture he walked, then made a quick slide under the electric fence and across the yard to Kenny's house. Up the steps on tiptoe, shoes squishing, he opened the screen door just a crack, and placed the gift on the doorstep. Taking a deep breath, he reached for the doorbell and pressed it hard.

Quickly, Marty turned, ran down the steps, and dashed across the yard in a wild race to get away unnoticed. Then, suddenly, he banged into the electric fence.

The shock sent him reeling. For a moment he lay stunned

on the wet ground. His body quivered and he gasped for breath. Then, slowly, weakly, confused and frightened, he began the grueling trip back home.

As he stumbled through the door, I hugged his muddy little body to me. He was still dazed, and a red mark began to blister on his face from his mouth to his ear. Quickly I treated it. With a warm cup of cocoa soothing him, Marty's bright spirits returned and I tucked him into bed.

That Christmas Eve I went to bed unhappy and puzzled. The accident with the fence seemed like such a cruel thing to happen to a little boy on the purest of Christmas missions. He was doing what the Lord wants us all to do . . . giving to others . . . and giving in secret at that.

I did not sleep well that night. Somewhere deep inside I think I was disappointed that Christmas Eve had been just an ordinary, problem-filled night, with no mysterious enchantment at all.

But I was wrong.

By morning the rain had stopped and the sun shone. The streak on Marty's face was very red, but I could tell that the burn was not serious. We opened our presents, and soon, not unexpectedly, Kenny knocked on the door, eager to show Marty his new compass and tell about the mystery of its arrival. It was plain that Kenny didn't suspect Marty. While the two of them talked, Marty just smiled and smiled.

Then I noticed that while the two boys compared their Christmases, nodding, gesturing and chattering away, Marty was not cocking his head. When Kenny talked, Marty seemed to listen with his deaf ear.

Weeks later a report came from the school nurse, verifying what Marty and I already knew. "Marty now has complete hearing in both ears."

The mystery of how Marty regained his hearing, and still has it, remains just that . . . a mystery. Doctors suspect, of course, that the shock from the electric fence was somehow responsible. Perhaps so. Whatever the reason, I just remain thankful to God for the good exchange of gifts that was made that night.

Diane Rayner, Guideposts, 12/83.

13

A Word about the Recipes In This Book . . .

The Scandinavians are known the world over for their Christmas celebrations and for their wonderful cooking and baking which is so much a part of a real Scandinavian traditional Christmas. I am one — I am 100 percent Norwegian. My father came to America as an immigrant when he was 18 years of age. He was on his way around the world but stopped in Minneapolis, Minnesota, to spend some time with his uncle. He stayed, he played professional soccer ball, met my mother, the two married, and the rest is history, as they say.

My mother's roots also come from Norway, as did her mother's family and her father's family. And so the traditions from that part of the world have molded our family's celebrations. My mother is known to her friends and family as a fabulous cook. I can attest firsthand to that endorsement. She has a way with an apron, mixing bowls, ovens, and love. Her own kids and their kids always looked forward with great delight to the special Christmas treats and feasts over which she presided with great joy and pride. Now it's another generation of great-grandkids who are growing to appreciate Grandma's cooking and baking.

When I began writing this book, I asked, "Mom, would

14

you be willing to now share some of those 'secret' family recipes with the readers of this book?"

There was some hesitation. You see, I was asking for gems that have not been shared with outsiders, even though many had asked for some of her secrets. It was like asking to be admitted to the inner chambers of Fort Knox. She replied, "Well, maybe it's time to share these. How many will you need?" There was a long pause, then she continued, "Well, since I'm well into my eighties, I'll let somebody else do some of the fussing for Christmas." Then she sat down with a pencil and pad to lovingly copy by hand all the recipes in this book.

So here you have them . . . some of the Strand/Steen/Jensen family secrets of Christmas cooking and baking. Neither Mom nor I can tell you where their origins have come from . . . some came from Norway and were translated into English, some from the head, some were evolved over time, some from my grandmother, some from experimentation, some came from my mother's sisters . . . but credit will go to Ruth Genavive Strand-Lundeen. I hope you enjoy them, because they have been time-tested by an appreciative audience of hungry participants and now carefully written out for you and yours to enjoy!

15

Julekage (Norwegian Christmas Bread)

2 cakes compressed yeast
1/2 cup lukewarm water
3 cups milk, scalded
1/2 cup butter
10 to 11 cups flour
2 teaspoons salt
1/2 teaspoon crushed cardamom seed

1/2 cup chopped citron
2 cups raisins
1/2 cup candied cherries (opt.)
1 cup sugar
2 eggs, beaten

METHOD: Dissolve yeast in water. Pour scalded milk over butter and when lukewarm add yeast, sugar, salt and about one half of flour. Beat well for 10 minutes. Add eggs, one at a time, beating thoroughly. Add fruit, cardamom, and enough flour to make a soft dough. Knead and place in greased bowl to rise until light, then knead and let rise again. Shape into five round loaves and place on greased pans to rise for about an hour or until light. Brush tops with egg yoke and milk mixture. Bake at 375 degrees for 45-50 minutes. After removing from oven, brush tops with melted butter and sprinkle with sugar and cinnamon.   (Ruth Strand-Lundeen)

16

The Lights of Christmas

At Christmas time there's no place half so treasured as one's own home, whose wreath-hung windowpanes and candle-lighted

sills show gladness and joy within. Light from the glowing chandelier and flaring logs add to the festive cheer and shimmer of the snow-draped world outside. Oh, home is very dear, at Christmas. Then, when the joy has left a mere, low flicker in my thoughts, I love to sit in quiet solitude and hear the clock tick intimately while I sit and meditate. Or read, or write a note or poem, or maybe sing a hymn in undertones, the carols which I lock deep in my heart, with every joyous, precious thing.

Bernice Anderson, adapted

The Candymaker's Witness

A candy maker in Indiana wanted to make a candy that would be a witness to Christmas so he made the **Christmas Candy Cane.** He incorporated several symbols for the birth, ministry, and death of Jesus Christ.

He began with a stick of pure white, hard candy. White was to symbolize the Virgin Birth and the sinless nature of Jesus Christ. It was hard to symbolize the Solid Rock . . . the foundation of the Church, and the firmness of the promises of God.

The candymaker made the candy in the form of a "J" to represent the precious name of Jesus who was born into this earth as our Saviour. It can also represent the staff of the "Good Shepherd" with which

18

He reaches down into the pits and ditches and holes of the world to lift out the fallen and hurting lambs, who, like sheep have gone astray.

Thinking that the candy cane was somewhat plain, the maker stained it with red stripes. He used the three small stripes to show the stripes laid on the back of Jesus at His trial and scourging. The large red strip was for the blood shed by Christ on the cross so that all of us could receive the promise of forgiveness which leads to eternal life.

Unfortunately, the candy became known as a "candy cane" which is now used as a meaningless decoration seen at Christmas time. But the next time you see or use or eat it, the meaning is still there for those who have "eyes to see and ears to hear." My prayer is that this simple, common symbol of Christmas will again be used to witness to the wonder and beauty of Jesus Christ and His great love that came down to all of us at Christmas!

19

Switching the Price Tags

Did you hear the true story about the characters who broke into a local downtown department store during the Christmas shopping season? They didn't steal a thing but must have had a blast switching price tags on the merchandise! The next morning when the customers arrived they were puzzled to find fur coats selling for $5.98 while a jar of cold cream was tagged for $375.00! In the jewelry department there were silver service sets tagged for $1.99 while umbrellas were tagged at $1,400.00! Diamond rings were tagged at $2.59 and head scarves were going for $9,995.00!

Perhaps you along with many others have been planning, shopping, decorating, shopping, baking, and more shopping as you are getting ready to celebrate Christmas. Before the final rush, let's pause a moment and ask ourselves: "Has something come into my life and switched the price tags? What really is important this Christmas? Have material things become more important than the gifts of the soul? Will I somehow misplace my priorities and love things while using people or will it be that I love people and use things?" And the bottom line question might be, "Where will Jesus Christ fit into your celebrating of His coming this year?"

His Name Is at the Top

I had the nicest Christmas list, the longest one in town,
Till Daddy looked at it and said, "You'll have to cut it down."

I knew that what he said was true
Beyond the faintest doubt,
But was amazed to hear him say,
"You've left your best Friend out."

And so I scanned my list again,
And said, "Oh, that's not true!"
But Daddy said, "His name's not there,
That Friend who died for you."

And then I clearly understood, 'twas Jesus that he meant;
For Him who should come first of all, I hadn't planned a cent!
I'd made a Christmas birthday list, and left the Saviour out!
But, oh, it didn't take me long to change the list about.

And tho' I've had to drop some names
Of folks I like a lot,
My Lord must have the most . . . because
His name is at the top!

The Laws of Physics and Santa Claus

NO KNOWN species of reindeer can fly. But there are some 300,000 species of living organisms yet to be classified. And while most of these are insects and germs, this does not COMPLETELY rule out flying reindeer, which only Santa has ever seen.

THERE ARE APPROXIMATELY TWO BILLION persons under 18 in the world. But since most of them do not include Santa Claus as part of their cultural traditions, let us suppose that Santa appears to only 15 percent of the total or about 378 million children according to the Population Reference Bureau. Let's take an average census rate of 3.5 children per household which calculates to 91.8 million homes. One must also presume that there is at least one good child in each home.

SANTA HAS only 31 hours of Christmas to work with, thanks to the different time zones and the rotation of the earth, assuming he travels from the east to the west (which seems logical). This works out to 822.6 visits per second. This is to say that for each of the 91.8 million homes, Santa has 1/1000 of a second to park, hop out of the sleigh, jump down the chimney, fill the stockings, distribute the remaining presents under the tree, eat

whatever snacks
have been left, get back into the sleigh, and
move on to the next house. Assuming that each of these 91.8
million stops are evenly distributed around the earth (which, of
course, we know to be false, but for the purposes of our calcula-
tions we will accept), we are now talking about .78 miles per
household, a total trip of 75 and 1/2 million miles, not counting
stops to do what most us must do at least once every 31 hours.

THIS MEANS THAT SANTA'S SLEIGH is moving at 650
miles per second . . . merely 3,000 times the speed of sound. For
purposes of comparison, the fastest man-made vehicle, the
Ulysses space probe, moves at a poky 27.4 miles per second. A
conventional reindeer can run, at tops, 15 miles per hour.

THE PAYLOAD ON THE SLEIGH adds another interest-
ing element. Assuming that each child gets nothing more than a
medium-sized "Lego" set (two pounds), the sleigh is carrying
321,300 tons, not counting Santa, who is invariably described
as overweight. On land, the conventional reindeer can pull no
more than 300 pounds. Even granting that "flying reindeer" could

pull ten times the normal amount, we cannot do the job with eight or even nine. We need 214,000 reindeer. This increases the payload . . . not even counting the weight of the sleigh . . . to 353,430 tons. Again, for comparison, this is four times the weight of the cruise ship Queen Elizabeth II.

THAT MANY TONS traveling at 650 miles per second creates enormous air resistance. This will heat the reindeer up in the same fashion as a spacecraft re-entering the earth's atmosphere. The lead pair of reindeer will absorb 14.3 QUINTILLION joules of energy . . . per second . . . each. In short, they will burst into flames almost instantaneously, exposing the reindeer behind them, and create deafening sonic booms in their wake. The entire reindeer team will be vaporized within 4.26 thousandths of a second. Santa, meanwhile, will be subjected to acceleration forces 17,500.06 times greater than gravity. A 250-pound Santa (which does seem ludicrously slim) would be pinned to the back of his sleigh by 4,315,015 pounds of force.

IN CONCLUSION . . . if Santa ever DID deliver all those presents on Christmas Eve, he's dead now!

It is Christmas in the heart that puts
Christmas in the air.   (W.T. Ellis)

Lefse

5 large potatoes
1/2 cup sweet cream
1 teaspoon salt
1/2 cup of flour to each cup of mashed potatoes

METHOD: Boil potatoes, mash very fine, then add cream, butter, and salt. Beat until light. Then let COOL. When cool, add flour (1/2 cup for each mashed potato), kneading until smooth. Roll into a long roll and slice in pieces about the size of a large egg. Roll each piece round as for a pie crust and thin as possible. Bake on lefse griddle or flat stove top until light brown, turning so as not to scorch.

SERVE with butter and brown sugar or butter and strawberry jam or butter and what have you that tastes good.

This is fabulous and a traditional "must" for every Norwegian Christmas celebration.

(Ruth Strand-Lundeen)

Creative Christmas Giving

Ray Collette already knows what he's getting for Christmas this year. It's the same pair of bothersome pants he's received every other year for the past ten years! But . . . he doesn't know where or how he'll find them!

The pants caper started when Collette's brother-in-law, Larry Kunkel, received a pair of mole-skin trousers one Christmas while he was a student at St. Cloud State University. He wore them a few times but they froze stiff in cold weather.

"He decided he didn't like them, so he gave them to me for Christmas the following year," Collette said. "I didn't like them, either, they were just miserable."

So the next Christmas, Collette neatly wrapped and packaged the bothersome pants and gave them back . . . the exchange has continued.

"After a couple of years, you got to the point where you knew you were going to get them," Collette said.

Collette decided to be creative so he twisted the pants tightly and stuffed them into a one-inch-wide tube. The following Christmas, Kunkel compressed them into a seven-inch square and wrapped them with wire. Not to be outdone, the next year,

Collette put the pants into a two-foot square crate filled with stones, nailed it shut, and banded it with steel. Kunkel retaliated by mounting the pants inside an insulated window that had a twenty-year guarantee and shipped the package off to Collette.

They were returned the next year in a five-inch coffee can soldered shut and placed in a five-gallon container filled with concrete and reinforcing rods. The following Christmas, Kunkel put them in a 225-pound, homemade ashtray, made from an eight-inch steel casing. Collette had to go to a repair shop where the ends were torched off and a 100-ton-hydraulic press was used to push out the inside steel casing that housed the trousers.

The next year Kunkel didn't receive them for Christmas. "He thought it's over," Collette said with a grin. But when Kunkel returned to work in Bensenville, Illinois, following the Christmas holiday, he found a red and green stripped 600-pound safe sitting in his office.

"I'm sure I'll get them back. I shudder to think of the things he might do," Collette said. But, he indicated that he's also made plans for years to come!

Now, how's that for a creative way to give? But for me, the most creative gift ever given was when God the Father packaged His Only Son in swaddling clothes and laid Him in a humble manger in Bethlehem!

Nativity

Something in the air tonight,
Lonely, strange, and holy.
Kings leave footprints in the sand,
Moving slowly, slowly.

Shepherds in their sheephide coats
Watch the star intently,
Speak to flocks with voices hushed,
Move them forward gently.

Time will hold its breath awhile,
Wind be still, be still,
Soft the flight of angel wings
Around this little hill.

Unto us a child is given,
Something strange and stranger . . .
the King of kings and Lord of lords,
An infant in a manger.

His name shall be called, Wonderful,
The Child is meek and lowly,
The Comforter, the Prince of Peace,
Holy, Holy, Holy.

— Marie Halbert King

Some of the Traditions of Christmas. . . .

SCORES of traditions and customs have grown up around the celebration of Christmas. Some honor Jesus Christ while others are secular, fantasy, or fun.

For cutting the first **Christmas tree**, the credit possibly should go to Martin Luther. The story is that while walking home on a clear, beautiful Christmas Eve, Luther cut down a tall evergreen. He took it home, propped it up, then topped it with lighted candles to symbolize the stars of the heaven which had shown so clearly on this night and he gave the tree as a surprise gift to his children.

The **Holly** that is universally used in Christmas decorations is grown in almost every country of the world and even bears fruit in winter. Some use holly to symbolize the "Crown of Thorns" with the red berries representing the blood of Jesus Christ which was shed for the world.

CHRISTMAS was called "Christes Masse" or "Christ's Mass" in jolly old medieval England until the two words were joined through common usage. In some European countries Christmas is called "Christ's Birthday." The French call the day "Noel" while the Italians say "Natale" and the Scandinavians "Yulen Jul."

The **Christmas gift giving** in Holland is kept on December 6 which is the day commemorating the day of the death of St. Nicholas. Their religious observance is then celebrated on December 25.

St. Nicholas was considered by Europeans to be the gift-bearing patron of children. Then Spanish influence in Holland changed "Saint" to "Santa." And there are many other names for Santa Claus: In Germany he is "Kris Kringle" and in France he is "Pere Noel" while in Scandinavia he is "Lady Befana." But children in Finland substitute a goat for Santa and the children of Italy have a woman as the gift giver of Christmas.

CHRISTMAS has not always been a legal holiday in the United States! In 1659 the Puritans managed to pass a Massachusetts "blue law" that levied a fine of four shillings on anyone caught celebrating Christmas. Fortunately, this law was on the books for only 22 years!

Lutefisk

You start by buying lutefisk at any butcher shop or grocery store that is brave enough to handle it.

Soak the lutefisk in cold water for 3 to 4 hours before using. Cut in serving size pieces. Place in cheese cloth and put on to boil in a kettle of cold water to which salt has been added. Cook about 5 minutes until fish is tender, then drain.

An alternative method is to bake in a medium oven in a covered casserole dish.

Serve with lots of hot melted butter or a cream sauce.

(Ruth Strand-Lundeen)

PS: If you survive the cooking and eating of lutefisk . . . you can consider yourself to have passed the initiation test required before anyone can become a full-fledged Norske!

A Norwegian/Irish Lutefisk Tale

One winter many years ago, the Vikings decided it was too cold in Norway and they wanted to stay somewhere warmer until spring. They went to Ireland, where they wore out their welcome real fast and threatened to eat the Irish out of house and home.

The Irish plotted to get rid of the Norwegians. So they pounded all of their potatoes flat to discourage the Vikings from eating them. But the Norwegians called that "lefse" (the flat potato bread, much like a tortilla, please refer to the lefse recipe in this book) and thought it was just fine.

Then the Irish decided to poison the Vikings. They poured lye all over their codfish supplies. But the hardy Norwegians just washed out the lye, called the dish "lutefisk" and thought it was just wonderful. This angered the Irish who snarled, "Why don't all you stubborn Norwegians just go to Hades?!" So they all moved to Minnesota and North Dakota.

On a note that is just a bit more serious . . . what is the big fuss about lutefisk? It's simply codfish that has been preserved with lye. Codfish without the lye treatment is called "torsk" in Norwegian. Yes, lutefisk has had lots of bad press, all well deserved . . . it stinks up the house, it turns the silverware black, and so forth. Incidentally, the lye in lutefisk is rinsed out in processing, leaving the codfish with a unique texture and some people think it tastes a bit like lobster, others think it's nothing but a disgusting, smelly glop! Oh, yes, Scandinavians aren't the only people who eat food that has been processed with lye. That southern delicacy, hominy grits, is made by using a lye bath to bleach the bran and germ out of whole corn kernels.

Well . . . so much for lutefisk. Try it, you might like it for your Christmas dinner!

On Christmas Eve, the story says, an enchantment falls upon the earth. The way to Christmas lies through an ancient gate, patterned after a sheepfold and guarded by angels with stardust in their hair. It is a little gate, child-high, child-wide, and there is a password: PEACE ON EARTH TO MEN OF GOOD WILL. May you, this Christmas, become as a little child again and enter into His kingdom.

(Angelo Patri)

Christmas Shopping

The time is early December. The place is the local shopping mall. The people are a family of four with lists in hand or head, readying to begin their shopping. The decision is made to shop separately so that the presents they purchase for each other will be kept secret until they are unwrapped. Before they split up, the father says, "Let's synchronize our watches and agree to meet at the car in the parking lot at five o'clock sharp." The four adjust their respective watches.

Then the mother turns to the father and with her hand outstretched, says, "Okay . . . now let's all synchronize our wallets!"

To see His star is good,
but to see His face is better.
(Dwight L. Moody)

Christmas is a time for exchanging a whole lot of things you can't afford for another whole lot of things you don't really want.

Swedish Meat Balls

1 pound of ground beef
2 teaspoons of salt
1/4 pound of ground pork sausage
1/4 teaspoon of pepper
1/2 cup milk
2 tablespoons of minced onions (sautéed)
1/2 cup bread crumbs
2 eggs

METHOD: Work all together until light and fluffy. Form into small balls and brown in skillet with butter.

Serve with brown gravy made from the drippings combined with 1 tablespoon of flour and 3/4 cup cream.

(Ruth Strand-Lundeen)

Sour Cream Twists

3-1/2 cups sifted Gold Medal Flour
3/4 cup thick sour cream (20%)
1 teaspoon salt
1 whole egg and 2 egg yolks (well beaten)
1 cup shortening (1/2 butter)
1 teaspoon vanilla
1 package active dry yeast
1 cup sugar
1/4 cup warm water

METHOD: Sift flour and salt into mixing bowl. Cut in shortening. Dissolve yeast in water. Stir into flour mixture with sour cream, eggs, and vanilla. Mix well by hand. Cover with damp cloth and refrigerate 2 hours.

Roll half of dough on sugared board, into an oblong 8" x 6". Fold ends to center with ends overlapping. Sprinkle with sugar, roll again to same size. Repeat a third time. Roll about 1/4 inch thick, cut into strips about 1" x 4". Twist ends in opposite directions, stretching dough slightly. Place strips on ungreased baking sheet or you can also shape them like horseshoes. Repeat with rest of dough. Bake in 375 degree oven about 15 minutes.

(Ruth Strand-Lundeen)

37

What Really Is Christmas?

Christmas is **MUSIC** . . . the music of carols ringing out on the still night air, the organ, the chimes, and the voices of a choir singing "Silent Night, Holy Night."

Christmas is **LIGHTS** . . . the candles in our windows, the lighted trees, the eyes of little children, and the starlight on a cold December night.

Christmas is **WELCOME** . . . the wreath on our door, the happiness to answer the doorbell, the warmth of hearts overflowing, "Come in, come in, and Merry Christmas!"

Christmas is **LAUGHTER** . . . the laughter that starts in our toes and bubbles up, the smiles on faces everywhere, the feeling of closeness, of a wonderful secret shared with all mankind.

Christmas is **FRAGRANCE** . . . the pine and spruce smell of Christmas trees, the sugary, good smell of cookies baking, the spice and raisin smell of fruitcake, the smell of furniture polish, and the cold, crisp smell outdoors.

Christmas is **GIVING** . . . the present made by hand, the card picked especially for a certain person, the gift marked from me to you with love.

Christmas is **REMEMBERING** . . . other Christmases, friends that may be far away, loved ones far and near, those less fortunate, those in need. To read again the words, "For God so loved. . . . " "Unto us a Son is born. . . . "

Christmas is **LOVE** . . . the love that wells up in our hearts and brings tears to our eyes as we thank God for His great love, His unspeakable Gift.

(Carol Bessent Hayman)

The Work of Christmas Begins

When the song of the angels is silent
When the star in the sky is gone
When the kings and princes are home
When the shepherd are again tending their sheep
When the manger is darkened and still
The work of Christmas begins . . .

>To find the lost
>>To heal the broken
>>>To feed the hungry
>>>>To rebuild the nations
>>To bring peace among people
>>>To befriend the lonely
>>>>To release the prisoner
>>>>>To make music in the heart.

(Howard Thurman)

40

A Christmas Gift

Some years ago, while conducting a series of meetings in Michigan City, I was asked to preach to the convicts in the state prison. I sat on the platform with the governor and watched the prisoners march in . . . 700 men, young and old. They marched in lock-step, every man's hand on the shoulder of the man before him. At the word of command they sat down. Among that number were 76 "lifers," men who had been committed to prison for life for the crime of murder.

After the singing I arose to preach, but could hardly speak for weeping. Disregarding all the rules of the prison, in my earnestness to help the poor, fallen men, I left the platform and walked down the aisle among them, taking one, and then another by the hand and praying for them. At the end of the row of men who were committed for murder, sat a man who, more than his fellows, seemed marked by sin's blighting curse. His face was seamed and rigid with scars and marks of vice and sin. He looked as though he might be a demon incarnate, if once aroused to anger. I placed my hand on his shoulder and wept and prayed with and for him.

When the service was over, the warden said to me, "Well, Kain, do you know you have broken the rules of the prison by leaving the platform?"

"Yes, sir, but I never can keep any rule while preaching. And I did want to get up close to the poor, despairing men and pray for them, and tell them of the love of Jesus the Saviour."

"Do you remember," asked the warden, "the man at the end of the line in the lifers row, whom you prayed with? Would you like to hear his history?"

"Yes," I answered.

"Well, here it is in brief:"

Tom Galson was sent here about eight years ago for the crime of murder. He was, without a doubt, one of the most desperate and vicious characters we had ever received, and, as was expected, gave us a great deal of trouble.

One Christmas Eve about six years ago, duty compelled me to spend the night at the prison instead of at home as I had anticipated. Early in the morning while it was yet dark, I left the prison for my home, my pockets full of presents for my little girl. It was a bitter cold morning and I buttoned my overcoat up to protect myself from the cutting wind that swept in from the lake. As I hurried along, I thought I saw somebody skulking in the shadow of the prison wall. I stopped and looked a little more closely and then I saw a little girl, wretchedly clothed in a thin dress; her bare feet thrust into a pair of shoes much the worse for wear. In her hand she held, tightly clasped, a small paper parcel. Wondering who she was and why she was out so early in the morning and yet too weary to be interested, I hurried on. But I soon heard that I was being followed. I stopped and turned around and there before me stood the same wretched-looking child.

"What do you want?" I asked sharply.

"Are you the warden of the prison, sir?"

"Yes, who are you, and why are you not at home?"

"Please, sir, I have no home. Mama died in the poorhouse two weeks ago, an' she told me just before she died that papa (Tom Galson) was in prison; an' she thought maybe he would like to see his little girl, now that mama is dead. Please, can't you let me see my papa? Today is Christmas and I want to give him a present."

"No," I replied gruffly, "you will have to wait until visitor's day," and started on.

I had not gone many steps when I felt a pull at my coat and a pleading voice said, "Please, don't go."

I stopped once more and looked into the pinched, beseeching face before me. Great tears were in her eyes, while her little chin quivered with emotion.

"Mister," she said, "if your little girl was me, and your little girl's mama had died in the poorhouse an' her papa was in prison, an' she had no place to go an' no one to love her, don't you think she would like to see her papa? If it was Christmas and your little girl came to see me, if I was warden of the prison, an' asked me to please let her see her papa to give him a Christmas present, don't you . . . don't you think I would say yes?"

By this time a great lump was in my throat and my eyes were swimming with tears. I answered, "Yes, my little girl, I think you would, and you shall see your papa."

Then taking her by the hand I hurried back to the prison, thinking of my own fair-haired little girl at home. Arriving in my office, I invited her to come near the warm stove while I sent a guard to bring prisoner #37 from his cell. As soon as he came into my office and saw the little girl his face clouded with an angry frown and in a gruff, savage tone he snapped:

"Nellie, what are you doing here; what do you want? Go back to your mother."

"Please, papa," sobbed the little girl, "Mama's dead. She died two weeks ago in the poorhouse, an' before she died she told me to take care of little Jimmie, 'cause you loved him so; an' told me to tell you she loved you, too . . . but, papa" and her voice broke in sobs and tears, "Jimmie died, too, last week, and now I am alone, Papa, an' today's Christmas, Papa, an' . . . an' I thought

44

maybe as you loved Jimmie, you would like a little Christmas present from him."

Here she unrolled the little package she held in her hand, until she came to a little package of tissue paper, from which she took out a little blonde curl and put it in her father's hand, saying as she did so, "I cut it from dear little Jimmie's head, Papa, just afore they buried him."

Number 37 by this time was sobbing like a child and so was I. Stooping down, #37 picked up the little girl, pressed her convulsively to his chest, while his great frame shook with suppressed emotion.

The scene was too sacred for me to look upon so I softly opened the door and left them alone. In about an hour I returned. #37 sat near the stove with his little daughter on his knee. He looked at me sheepishly for a moment and then said, "Warden, I haven't any money." Then suddenly stripping off his prison jacket, said, "For God's sake, don't let my little girl go out this bitter cold day with that thin dress. Let me give her this coat. I'll work early and late, I'll do anything. I'll be a man. Please, Warden, let me cover her with this coat." Tears were streaming down the face of that hardened man.

"No, Galson," I said, "keep your coat, your little girl will not suffer. I'll take her and see what my wife can do for her."

"God bless you," sobbed Galson.

I took the little girl to my home. She has remained with us all these years and has become a true Christian by expressing her faith in the Lord Jesus Christ. Tom Galson also became a Christian and has become a model prisoner and has given us no more trouble.

Some years later when I visited the prison again, the Warden said to me, "Kain, would you like to see Tom Galson, whose story I told you a few years ago?"

"Yes, I would," I answered.

The Warden took me down a quiet street and stopping at a neat little home, knocked at the door. The door was opened by a cheerful young lady, who greeted the Warden with a warm hug of welcome.

We went on in and then the Warden introduced me to Nellie and her father, Tom Galson. Because of his reformation he had been granted a pardon and was now living an upright Christian, productive life with his daughter . . . Nellie, whose little Christmas gift had broken his hard heart and started the turnaround in his life.

Kain, *The King's Herald*, printed in *Full Gospel Tidings*, 12/42, and reprinted in 12/72.

A Child Is Born

That holy night when stars shone bright,
Our hearts beat high with joy;
A baby's birth upon the earth,
Held hope without alloy.

    Shepherds in fright made hasty flight,
    And sped to the stable bed;
    They kneeled to pray where the baby lay
    And worshiped the hallowed head.

        Three kings so wise beheld the skies,
        They saw a moving star;
        It guided them to Bethlehem,
        From distant lands afar.

            O blessed morn a child is born,
            In a manger on the hay;
            Let angels sing, hosannas ring,
            A King has come today.

                (Unknown)

☆
THERE is
a legend
that tells that
when Jesus was
born the sun danced
in the sky, the aged trees
straightened themselves
and put on leaves and sent
forth the fragrance of blossoms
once more. These are the symbols of
what takes place in our hearts when the
Christ Child is born anew each year. Blessed
by the Christmas sunshine, our natures, perhaps
long leafless, bring forth new love, new kindness,
new mercy, new compassion. As the birth of Jesus was
the beginning of the Christian life, so the unselfish joy at
Christmas shall start the spirit that is to rule the New Year.

Helen
Keller,
The
Miracle
of
Christmas,
Hallmark
Cards

The Prophet's Promise

THE PEOPLE walking in darkness have seen a great light; on those living in the land of the shadow of death a light has dawned. You have enlarged the nation and increased their joy; they rejoice before you as people rejoice at the harvest, as men rejoice when dividing the plunder.

FOR as in the day of Midian's defeat, you have shattered the yoke that burdens them, the bar across their shoulders, the rod of their oppressor.

Every warrior's boot used in battle and every garment rolled in blood will be destined for burning, will be fuel for the fire.

FOR UNTO US a child is born, to us a son is given, and the government will be on his shoulders. And He will be called wonderful counselor, mighty God, everlasting father, Prince of Peace.

OF THE INCREASE OF HIS GOVERNMENT AND PEACE there will be no end. He will reign on David's throne and over his kingdom, establishing and upholding it with justice and righteousness from that time on and forever!

The zeal of the LORD ALMIGHTY will accomplish this!

(Isa. 9:2-7;NIV).

The Modern Understanding

Lester Weeks, pastor of the First Christian Church of Platte City, Missouri, relates this story: "Last November my choir director asked me if I would pick up the sheet music for 'How Great Thou Art.' I happened to be in the shopping center the next day, so I went in a record store and asked the clerk, 'Do you carry any religious sheet music?'

"The clerk (she looked like a high school student) thought a moment and then said: 'Some of the Christmas music might be religious.'"

Lester Weeks, *Parables, Etc.*, 12/83

In the Spirit of Giving

During the Christmas season of 1981, a story was carried by UPI which appeared across the country illustrating the real holiday spirit of giving. Craig Bartlett of White Bear Lake, Minnesota was in desperate need of a different car than the one he had been driving. But all he had managed to accumulate was

$100. Yet, he and his family headed out in search of another car. However, before he got to town in his dilapidated heap it broke down, leaving them stuck on the edge of town, a number of blocks from their destination.

With no other choice, he and his wife bundled their children (ages two and five) up in blankets and started walking. They finally made their way to their destination, a used car lot. Then he hesitatingly, haltingly, embarrassed asked if by chance they had a car to sell to him for $100.

The salesman said, "I am sorry. We have no cars to sell for $100 but we do have one we will sell you, that hopefully you can afford. It's priced at $6.50! (One dollar for the notary and $5.50 for the transfer fee.)"

The Bartletts were speechless! The owner of the lot had seen them coming down the road, a pitiful sight in the dead of a Minnesota winter, and was touched by their plight and decided to give them a car!

Then the owner said, "Take the balance of the $100 and buy some things for the children for their Christmas!" WHAT A CHRISTMAS THAT WAS! And my suspicions are that the owner of the used car lot had the best of the joys of Christmas!

51

THE FOLLOWING IS A FABULOUS FOUR-STAR DESSERT!

Norwegian Rum Pudding

4 egg yolks
1 tablespoon rum flavoring or
    a few drops of rum extract
4 tablespoons sugar
1 tablespoon knox gelatin
2 cups of cream, whipped

METHOD: Soak gelatin in 1/3 cup cold water, then melt over hot water. Stir egg yolks and sugar together, then add to the whipped cream with flavoring, pour into a ring mold and let it set until firm. Unmold on fancy plate, decorate with fresh fruit or serve with the described crimson raspberry sauce.

CRIMSON RASPBERRY SAUCE: Thaw and crush one 10-ounce package of frozen red raspberries. Combine with 1-1/2 teaspoons cornstarch, add 1/2 cup red currant jelly. Bring to boiling cook and stir until mixture is clear and thickens slightly. Strain and chill. Makes about 1-1/3 cups.

(Ruth Strand-Lundeen)

The Short Version

A small boy who was in a Christmas program had but one sentence to say: "Behold, I bring you good tidings." After the rehearsal he asked his mother what "tidings" meant and she told him it meant "news."

When the program was being presented, he was stage-struck and forgot his line. As he was thinking hard, speechless, finally the idea came back to him and he shouted out: "Hey, I got news for you!"

The Gift of the Magi

At about the turn of this century. . . .

A story is told about a young married couple whose names are Jim and Della. They are poor but very much in love with each other.

As Christmas approaches, Della wonders what to get Jim for Christmas. She would like to give him a watch chain for his gold watch, but she doesn't have enough money. Then she gets an idea. She has beautiful long hair. So Della decides to cut off her hair and sell it to buy the fancy chain for Jim's watch.

On Christmas Eve she returns home, and in her hand is a beautiful box containing a gold watch chain which she purchased by selling her hair. Suddenly Della begins to worry. She knows Jim admired her long hair, and she wonders if he will be disappointed that she cut it off and sold it.

Della climbs the final flight of stairs leading to their tiny apartment. She unlocks the door and is surprised to find Jim home and waiting for her. In his hand is a neatly wrapped box containing his gift he purchased for her.

When Della removes her scarf, Jim sees Della's short hair, and tears well up in his eyes. But he says nothing. He chokes back the tears and gives Della the gift box.

When Della opens it, she can't believe her eyes. There in the box is a set of beautiful silver combs for her long hair.

And when Jim opens his gift, he, too, is astonished. There inside the box is a beautiful gold chain for his gold pocket watch. Only then does Della realize that Jim pawned his gold watch to buy her the silver hair combs.

Far more beautiful than the gifts is the love they symbolize.

(O. Henry, adapted)

The challenge of simplicity is a magnet to the human spirit. Much of the beauty of Christmas lies in its challenge to look further, deeper, until we find its secret in the heart of God.

(Dale Evans Rogers)

Powerful Grasp

Christmas is love
tugging man back to God
With the powerful grasp
of a tiny hand
Reaching out from a bed of straw.

(Molly Brown)

Silent Night

There is a powerful book, *Life and Death in Shanghai*, written by Nien Cheng which contains the amazing story of a Chinese woman who was arrested and spent seven long years in solitary confinement during the Cultural Revolution in communist China. It's a fascinating story of endurance and faith in the face of persecution. The following is an excerpt describing an experience of joy and hope in the midst of the darkness:

When the newspaper stopped coming on December 2, I started to make light scratches on the wall to mark the passing days. By the time I had made 23 strokes, I knew it was Christmas Eve. Though the usual bedtime hour had passed, the guards were not yet on duty to tell the prisoners to go to sleep. While I was waiting in the bitter cold, suddenly, from somewhere upstairs, I heard a young soprano voice singing, at first tentatively and then boldly, the Chinese version of "Silent Night." The prison walls resounded with her song as her clear and melodious voice floated in and out of the dark corridors. I was enraptured and deeply moved as I listened to her. I knew from the way she rendered the song that she was a professional singer who had incurred the displeasure of the Maoists.

No concert I had attended at Christmas in any year meant more to me than that moment when I sat in my icy cell listening to "Silent Night" sung by another prisoner whom I could not see. As soon as she was confident that the guards were not there to stop her, the girl sang beautifully without any trace of nervousness. The prison became very quiet. All the inmates listened to her with baited breath.

Nien Cheng, *Life and Death in Shanghai* (New York, NY: Grove Press, 1986).

The Christmas Bells

This story concerns the bells of a famous church in a far-off country, in a faraway time. It is an old story, one of those classic stories of Christmas which have been told and retold from generation to generation. And it's worth reading again because of its beauty and truth.

THESE AMAZING BELLS in the church tower were known all over the globe for the rare beauty of their chimes . . . it was said that their sound was the sweetest melody in all the world. *Because the music of the bells was so wonderful, they rang only on Christmas, never on ordinary occasions.* So it became the custom in that country for people to come from everywhere on Christmas Eve to the great church with its glorious Christmas bells. They would bring generous offerings and lay them on the altar . . . it was only at this moment of sacrificial giving that the Christmas bells would be heard. WHO RANG THEM, NO ONE KNEW! It was said that mysterious angelic hands pulled the bell rope and the lovely sound would float out filling the air with melody until the church was engulfed in entrancing beauty.

STRANGELY, however, despite the great reputation of the

bells and their music, probably no living soul had ever heard them. Their lovely sound was known only by tradition, because for long years the bells had not rung. This was due to the fact that the people had become neglectful of the church and indifferent to God. The gift offerings were growing smaller and none had recently been great enough to cause the bells to ring. And so their beauty was remembered only as fathers handed down the story to their children. Only in memory did their wonder remain!

Eventually this situation became something of a national scandal and the king himself took the question in hand. He decided one Christmas that EVERYONE should be encouraged to bring to the church the best and most generous gifts they could find. The king said that he would personally bring his own gift to the church on Christmas Eve. Naturally, everyone planned to visit the city for this great event!

No one made plans more carefully than two little boys who lived a long distance into the country. These two children were sons of a poor family, but somehow each managed to earn and save a small silver coin for an offering. Early on the afternoon before Christmas, holding the coins tightly so they would not be lost, they started their long walk to the city and the church.

It was bitterly cold and they had not gone very far before it started to snow heavily. But they did not let that stop them and hand in hand, their shabby clothes wrapped tightly about them, they trudged through the snow. Evening was coming on and it was growing dark, but they could see throngs hurrying to the church.

SUDDENLY . . . the older boy stumbled on a dark object huddled in the snow. Kneeling down to investigate, he was startled to find an old woman, half-frozen, but still alive. He lifted her and began to rub her wrists and temples. The woman's breathing grew more regular and he redoubled his efforts. As the boy worked at his task of human love and service, the lights of the city streets came on and immense crowds could be seen converging toward the church. The older boy looked up at his brother, "YOU go on to church," he said, handing him his treasured bit of silver. "Here's my offering. I must stay and do what I can to help this poor woman!"

Reluctantly, the younger boy set off alone, the two small pieces clutched in his hand. When he reached the church it was very crowded and the ceremony had started. Being small of stature, like boys, he managed to squeeze his way through the crowd to find a place near the front where he could see everything.

People were already beginning to bring their gifts to the altar . . . the gifts grew richer and more impressive and more luxurious as time passed. BUT THE BELLS REMAINED SILENT!

Finally, the king himself stood at the altar, resplendent in his magnificent robes and the jewelry of state. With a dramatic gesture he took his gold crown from his head and placed it on the altar . . . everyone waited expectantly . . . surely bells would ring for this magnificent and sacrificial gift. But no sound was heard.

Sadly, the king turned to walk down the aisle and leave the church . . . the people began to follow him. THEN, SUDDENLY, FROM SOMEWHERE HIGH IN THE VAULTED ARCHES OF THE CHURCH, THE MOST HEAVENLY MUSIC BEGAN TO RING OUT!

The tumultuous sound of the glorious Christmas bells filled the frosty air . . . the huge crowd stood transfixed. Then everyone looked back at the altar, but there was no one there!

NO ONE, THAT IS, BUT A SMALL BOY SHYLY PUTTING TWO TINY SILVER COINS ON THE ALTAR NEAR THE KING'S CROWN!

(Raymond MacDonald Alden)

Orange-Eggnog Float Punch

3 eggs
1/4 cup lemon juice
3 tablespoons sugar
1 pint vanilla ice cream
2 1/2 cups ice water
1 small bottle (1 cup) ginger ale
2 6 oz. cans frozen orange juice
    concentrate

METHOD: Beat eggs and sugar together until light and lemon colored. Stir in water, orange concentrate, and lemon juice. Place small scoops of ice cream in punch bowl and pour juice mixture over. Just before serving, add ginger ale. Makes about 10 servings.

(Ruth Strand-Lundeen)

SEASON'S GREETINGS

FELICES FIESTAS

JOYEAUX NOEL

FROHES WEIHNACHTSFEST

A Bed In My Heart

Ah, dearest Jesus, Holy Child,

Make Thee a bed, soft, undefiled,

Within my heart, that it may be

A quiet chamber kept for Thee.

My heart for very joy doth leap,

My lips no more can silence keep.

I, too, must sing, with joyful tongue,

That sweetest ancient cradle song,

Glory to God in highest heaven,

Who unto man His Son hath given,

While angels sing with pious mirth,

A glad New Year to all the earth.

(Martin Luther)

Fatigman

(Norwegian Poor Man's Cake)
3 eggs
3 tablespoons sugar
3 tablespoons sweet cream
pinch of salt
flavoring of your choice
flour as needed

METHOD: Beat together and add enough flour to roll very thin. Cut into diamond shapes with slit in center. Drop into hot oil and cook until a light brown. You can dust them with powdered sugar, dip them in brightly colored sugars, or eat them plain. Very tasty.

(Ruth Strand-Lundeen)

Heap on more wood! . . .
The wind is chill;
but let it whistle as it will,
we'll keep our Christmas merry still!

(Sir Walter Scott)

A Prayer
for Christmas Morning

THE DAY OF JOY RETURNS,
FATHER IN HEAVEN, AND
CROWNS ANOTHER YEAR
WITH PEACE AND GOOD WILL.
HELP us rightly to remember the birth of Jesus,
that we may share in the song of the angels,
the gladness of the shepherds,
and the worship of the wisemen.
Close the doors of hate and open the doors of
love all over the world. . . .
Let kindness come with every gift and good
desires with every greeting.
Deliver us from evil, by the blessing that Christ brings,
and teach us to be merry with clean hearts.

May this Christmas morning make us happy to be your
children, and this Christmas evening bring us to our bed with
grateful thoughts, forgiving and forgiven, for Jesus' sake.

AMEN.

God Came Down to Us

The depths of human humility to which Jesus stooped when He came to this earth in the most humble of all circumstances was thrust quite suddenly upon the consciousness of a missionary who was being held captive by the Chinese Communists. He writes the following:

After a meal and when it was already dark, it was necessary for me to go downstairs to give more hay to the horses. Chien permitted my going and I clambered down the notched tree trunk to the lower floor, which was given over in the usual manner to stabling. Below, it was absolutely pitch black. My boots squelched in the manure and straw on the floor and the fetid smell of the animals was nauseating. I felt my way among the mules and horses, expecting to be kicked at any moment. *What a place,* I thought.

Then, as I continued to grope my way in the darkness toward the gray, it suddenly flashed into my mind, *What's today?*

I thought for a moment. In traveling, the days had become a little muddled in my mind. Then it came to me, *It's Christmas Eve!* I stood still, suddenly still, in that oriental manger. To think that my Saviour was born in a place like this. To think that He came all the way from heaven to some wretched Eastern stable and, what is more, to think that He came for me. How men beautify the cross and crib, as if to hide the fact that at birth we resigned Him to the stench of beasts, and at death exposed Him to the shame of rogues. God forgive us.*

Love to the uttermost, love to the uttermost,
    Love past all measuring His love must be;
        From Heaven's highest glory to earth's deepest shame,
        This is the love of my Saviour to me.

(Unknown)

*(Geoffrey T. Bull, *When Iron Gates Yield.*)

This is Christmas: not the tinsel, not the giving and receiving, not even the carols, but the humble heart that receives anew the wondrous gift, the Christ! (Frank McKibben)

67

A Letter to Santa from a Mother

DEAR SANTA CLAUS:

You'll probably be surprised to receive this letter from an adult. You may be even more surprised as you read it to find that the writer is neither a maiden aunt nor a disgruntled bachelor. I'm a young mother.

It isn't my intention, Santa, to hurt your feelings. You see, my family has paid tribute to you for many past Christmases: my husband and I when we were in our childhood, and now our children who are six, four, and one. They still care for you. How much they care has really proved a problem in recent years. It is threatening to happen again this holiday season.

Our children worship you. They speak of you constantly. They watch diligently for your December 25 appearance. Can you tell us, Santa, what you have done to deserve this faithfulness from two generations? Can you promise any future consideration in exchange for past loyalties?

During a family crisis, have you ever told us, "I am with you always?" Were you ever with us during sorrow to comfort us with these words: "But your sorrow will be turned into joy?" And, Santa, there have been doubtful times. Where were you?

We didn't hear the calming message: "I will never leave you, nor forsake you."

We have come to the conclusion that you have been even less than a friend should be. And we have been shortchanged. My three children have stood on a windy, cold Main Street just to get a glimpse of your jolly face. They have written heartfelt yearly letters. They have gone to department stores to whisper in your ear. They have worked hard at being good in anticipation of your Christmas Eve visits. Yes, they've done all this . . . as their father and I did before them.

But there's going to be a change this Christmas. There isn't going to be any Santa Claus worship in our home. We've decided to focus our attention and adoration on another being . . . One who has stood by us the other 364 days this past year; One who has comforted us during the sorrowful and doubtful times . . . and, yes, the times of crisis, also.

It's true that your name will probably be mentioned around our house, Santa. Old habits are hard to break abruptly. But someone else's name will be mentioned much more often. The children will probably work just as hard at being good, but I hope they will do it for another inducement . . . one that will last the whole year long . . . to bring glory to another's name. That other One has given us so much more . . . and not just on Christmas Eve!

You may call our family fickle, Santa, but we won't mind. On this December 25, and all through the coming year, we want a Comforter, a Healer, a strengthening King. We don't want a myth any longer.

You see, our Christmas thoughts will revolve around a manger and a tiny Baby wrapped in swaddling clothes. We've talked it over. This year we've decided to give tribute, honor, and worship to Someone who really deserves them . . . to the True Giver . . . our God and Saviour.

Farewell, A Young Mother

Ann Lamp, The Greenville News, 12/72.

What Do You Do with Jesus at Christmas?

The kids were putting on the Christmas play. To show the radiance of the new born Saviour, an electric light bulb was hidden in the manger. All the stage lights were to be turned off so that only the brightness of the manger could be seen, but the boy who controlled the light got confused . . . all the lights went out!

It was a tense moment . . . broken only when one of the shepherds said in a loud stage whisper, "Hey! You switched off Jesus!"   (William Stehr)

Rolled Christmas Sugar Cookies

Ruth says, "This is a very easy cookie recipe which is more than 80 years old."

4 cups flour
2 eggs beaten
1 teaspoon baking powder
1 teaspoon soda
1 cup shortening (half butter)
1/3 cup milk
1 heaping cup sugar
1 teaspoon vanilla
1/2 teaspoon salt

METHOD: Mix flour, baking powder, salt, and shortening as for a pie crust. In another bowl add the soda and sugar, blend well, then add beaten eggs, milk, and vanilla. Pour the sugar mixture into the flour mixture and mix until smooth. Roll out on a floured board and cut into desired shapes using Christmas cookie cutters. Bake in moderate hot oven of 375 degrees about 8 to 10 minutes. Frost and decorate as desired.

(Ruth Strand-Lundeen)

Picking the Right Christmas Tree

It was a crisp, sunny afternoon in late November and we were searching for a tree at the Christmas tree farm. We always relish the task, as members of the family comb the farm for the perfect tree. (Not too tall, not too thin, just the right shape, and, of course, a straight trunk!) As were looking, we came upon the Marshes, dear friends of ours from church. I remarked, "This place is filled with beautiful trees! It is going to be hard to pick one!"

Jeanine Marsh replied, "Not for me. I never look for perfect trees! I'm looking for a tree that needs me! Then I'll make it beautiful!"*

As I wrote this it struck me . . . God is doing the same thing! And I'm so glad He is! Think of some of the people God has chosen who needed Him. He's not seeking for perfection or none of us would be chosen, including me. When we realize this truth and the process . . . then God can make something beautiful of our lives. What a gift at Christmas to receive!

*(Todd Jones)

72

Before Christ, a man loves things and uses people. After Christ, he loves people and uses things. (Horace Wood)

Christmas living is the best kind of Christmas giving! (Van Dyke)

The best of all gifts around any Christmas tree: the presence of a happy family all wrapped up in each other. (Burton Hillis)

To believe that the spirit of Christmas does change lives and to labor for the realization of its coming to all men is the essence of our faith in Christ. (William Parks)

Christmas began in the heart of God. It is complete only when it reaches the heart of man. (Religious Telescope)

The Light that shines from the humble manger is strong enough to lighten our way to the end of our days. (Vita-Rays)

The Revelation on Christmas Eve

One CHRISTMAS EVE singer Ira D. Sankey was traveling by steamboat up the Delaware River. The captain, aware of who Mr. Sankey was, had asked him to sing for the passengers during the supper time. Mr. Sankey then sang the "Shepherd Song." After the song was finished, a man with a rough, weatherbeaten face came up to Mr. Sankey and asked, "Did you ever serve in the Union Army?"

Sankey replied, "Yes, I did."

The man asked, "Can you remember if you were doing picket duty on a bright moonlight night in 1862?"

Sankey, surprised, said, "Yes, I did."

The stranger went on, "So did I. But I was serving in the Confederate army. When I saw you standing at your post, I said to myself: 'That fellow will never get away from here alive.' I raised my rifle and took aim. I was standing in the shadow completely concealed, while the full light of the moon was falling upon you.

"At that instant, just as a few moments ago, you raised your eyes to heaven and began to sing. Music, especially song, has always had a wonderful power over me and I took my finger off the trigger. 'Let him sing his song to the end,' I said to myself. 'I can shoot him afterwards. He's my victim at all events and my bullet cannot miss him.' But the song you sang then was the same song you sang just now. I heard the words perfectly:

> We are Thine, do Thou befriend us
> Be the guardian of our way. . . .

"Those words stirred up many memories in my heart. I began to think of my childhood and my God-fearing mother. She had many, many times sung that song to me. But she died all too soon, otherwise much in my life would no doubt have been different.

"When you had finished your song it was impossible for me to take aim at you again. I thought: *The Lord who is able to save that man from certain death must surely be great and mighty,* and my arm of its own accord dropped limp at my side."

Author unknown, from Religious Digest

75

I Am the Christmas Spirit

I enter the home of poverty, causing pale-faced children to open their eyes wide, in pleased wonder.

I cause the miser's clutched hand to relax and thus paint a bright spot on his soul.

I cause the aged to renew their youth and to laugh in the old glad way.

I keep romance alive in the heart of childhood, and brighten sleep with dreams woven of magic.

I cause eager feet to climb dark stairways with filled baskets, leaving behind hearts amazed at the goodness of the world.

I cause the prodigal to pause a moment on his wild, wasteful way and send to anxious love some little token that releases glad tears . . . tears which wash away the hard lines of sorrow.

I enter dark prison cells, reminding scarred manhood of what might have been and pointing forward to good days yet to be.

I come softly into the still white home of pain, and lips that are too weak to speak, just tremble in silent, eloquent gratitude.

In a thousand ways, I cause the weary world to look up into

the face of God, and for a little moment forget the things that are small and wretched.

I AM THE CHRISTMAS SPIRIT!

(E. C. Baird)

Real Christmas Giving

Several years ago a 13-year-old boy who attended Mohawk Central School at Paines Hollow in New York heard an appeal for contributions to Santa Claus Anonymous, a group that provides gifts for unfortunate children who otherwise would go without Christmas presents. The boy struggled to acquire and save a few pennies for this purpose. On the Friday before Christmas vacation he had 15 cents and planned to turn in this small treasure at the school that day. But a furious blizzard blasted the area that Friday and the school buses could not run. So the boy waded a considerable distance through deep snow to give his 15 cents to the school principal.

The principal found it difficult to control his emotions as he accepted the gift . . . for the youngster was one of the destitute children listed to receive a Christmas present from Santa Claus Anonymous.　(Harold Kohn, *The Tinsel and the Hay*)

Christmas Day in the Morning

He woke suddenly and completely. It was four o'clock, the hour at which his father had always called him to get up and help with the milking. Strange how the habits of his youth clung to him still! Fifty years ago (and his father had been dead for 30), and yet he waked at four o'clock in the morning. He had trained himself to turn over and go to sleep, but this morning it was Christmas; he did not try to sleep.

Yet what was the magic of Christmas now? His childhood and youth were long past, and his own children had grown up and gone. Some of them lived only a few miles away, but they had their own families, and though they would come in as usual toward the end of the day, they had explained with infinite gentleness that they wanted their children to build Christmas memories about *their* houses, not his. He was left alone with his wife.

Yesterday she had said, "It isn't worthwhile, perhaps. . . ."

And he had said, "Oh, yes, Alice, even if there are only the two of us, let's have a Christmas of our own."

Then she had said, "Let's not trim the tree until tomorrow, Robert . . . just so it's ready when the children come. I'm tired."

He had agreed, and the tree was still out in the back entry.

78

He lay in his big bed in his room. The door to her room was shut because she is a light sleeper, and sometimes he had restless nights. Years ago they had decided to use separate rooms. It meant nothing, they said, except that neither of them slept as well as they once had. They had been married so long that nothing could separate them, actually.

Why did he feel so awake tonight? For it was a still night, a clear and starry night. No moon, of course, but the stars were extraordinary! Now that he thought of it, the stars seemed always large and clear before the dawn of Christmas Day. There was one star now that was certainly larger and brighter than any of the others. He could even imagine it moving, as it had seemed to him to move one night long ago.

He slipped back in time, as he did so easily nowadays. He was 15 years old and still on his father's farm. He loved his father. He had not known it until one day a few days before Christmas, when he had overheard what his father was saying to his mother.

"Mary, I hate to call Rob in the mornings. He's growing so fast and he needs his sleep. If you could see how he sleeps when I go in to wake him up! I wish I could manage alone."

"Well, you can't, Adam." His mother's voice was brisk. "Besides, he isn't a child any more. It's time he took his turn."

"Yes," his father said slowly. "But I sure hate to wake him."

When he heard those words, something in him woke: His father loved him! He had never thought of it before, taking for granted the tie of their blood. Neither his father nor his mother talked about loving their children . . . they had no time for such things. There was always so much to do on a farm.

Now that he knew his father loved him, there would be no more loitering in the mornings and having to be called again. He got up after that, stumbling blind with sleep, and pulled on his clothes, his eyes tight shut, but he got up.

And then on the night before Christmas, that year when he was 15, he lay for a few minutes thinking about the next day. They were poor, and most of the excitement was in the turkey they had raised themselves and in the mince pies his mother made. His sisters sewed presents and his mother and father always bought something he needed, not only a warm jacket, maybe, but something more, such as a book. And he saved and bought them each something, too.

He wished, that Christmas he was 15, he had a better present for his father. As usual he had gone to the ten-cent store and bought a tie. It had seemed nice enough until he lay thinking the night before Christmas, and then he wished that he had heard his father and mother talking in time for him to save for something better.

He lay on his side, his head supported by his elbow, and looked out of his attic window. The stars were bright, much brighter than he ever remembered seeing them, and one star in particular was so bright that he wondered if it were really the Star of Bethlehem.

"Dad," he had once asked when he was a little boy, "what is a stable?"

"It's just a barn," his father had replied, "like ours."

Then Jesus had been born in a barn, and to a barn the shepherds had come, bringing their Christmas gifts!

The thought struck him like a silver dagger. Why should he not give his father a special gift too, out there in the barn? He could get up early, earlier than four o'clock, and he could creep into the barn and get all the milking done. He'd do it alone, milk and clean up, and then when his father went in to start the milking, he'd see it all done. And he would know who had done it.

He laughed to himself as he gazed at the stars. It was what he would do, and he mustn't sleep too sound.

He must have waked 20 times, scratching a match each time to look at his old watch . . . midnight, and half past one, and then two o'clock.

At a quarter to three he got up and put on his clothes. He crept downstairs, careful of the creaky boards, and let himself out. The big star hung lower over the barn roof, a reddish gold. The cows looked at him, sleepy and surprised. It was early for them, too.

"So, boss," he whispered. They accepted him placidly and he fetched some hay for each cow and then got the milking pail and the big milk cans.

He had never milked all alone before, but it seemed almost easy. He kept thinking about his father's surprise. His father would come in and call him, saying that he would get things started while Rob was getting dressed. He'd go to the barn, open the door, and then he'd go to get the two big empty milk cans. But they wouldn't be waiting or empty; they'd be standing in the milkhouse, filled.

"What the . . . " he could hear his father exclaiming.

He smiled and milked steadily, two strong streams rushing into the pail, frothing and fragrant. The cows were still surprised but acquiescent. For once they were behaving well, as though they knew it was Christmas.

The task went more easily than he had ever known it to before. Milking, for once, was not a chore. It was something else — a gift to his father who loved him. He finished, the two milk cans were full, and he covered them and closed the milkhouse door carefully, making sure of the latch. He put the stool in its place by the door and hung up the clean milk pail. Then he went out of the barn and barred the door behind him.

Back in his room he had only a minute to pull off his clothes in the darkness and jump into bed, for he heard his father up. He put the covers over his head to silence his quick breathing. The door opened.

"Rob!" his father called. "We have to get up, son, even if it is Christmas."

"Aw-right," he said sleepily.

"I'll go on out," he father said. "I'll get things started."

The door closed and he lay still, laughing to himself. In just a few minutes his father would know. His dancing heart was ready to jump from his body.

The minutes were endless . . . 10, 15, he did not know how

many . . . and he heard his father's footsteps again. The door opened and he lay still.

"Rob!"

"Yes, Dad. . . ."

"You, son of. . . ." His father was laughing a queer sobbing sort of laugh. "Thought you'd fool me, did you?" His father was standing beside his bed, feeling for him, pulling away the cover.

"It's for Christmas, Dad!"

He found his father and clutched him in a great hug. He felt his father's arms go around him. It was dark and they could not see each other's faces.

"Son, I thank you. Nobody ever did a nicer thing. . . ."

"Oh, Dad, I want you to know. . . . I do want to be good!"

The words broke from him of their own will. He did not know what to say. His heart was bursting with love.

"Well, I reckon I can go back to bed and sleep," he father said after a moment. "No, listen . . . the little ones are waked up. Come to think of it, son, I've never seen you children when you first saw the Christmas tree. I was always in the barn. Come on!"

He got up and pulled on his clothes again and they went down to the Christmas tree, and soon the sun was creeping up to where the star had been. Oh, what a Christmas, and how his heart had nearly burst again with shyness and pride as his father told his mother and made the younger children listen about how he, Rob, had got up all by himself.

"The best Christmas gift I ever had, and I'll remember it, son, every year on Christmas morning, so long as I live."

They had both remembered it, and now that his father was dead he remembered it alone: that blessed Christmas dawn when, alone with the cows in the barn, he had made his first gift of true love.

Outside the window now the great star slowly sank. He got up out of bed and put on his slippers and bathrobe and went softly upstairs to the attic and found the box of Christmas tree decorations. He took them downstairs into the living room. Then he brought in the tree. It was a little one . . . they had not had a big tree since the children went away . . . but he set it in the holder and put it in the middle of the long table under the window. Then carefully he began to trim it.

It was done very soon, the time passing as quickly as it had that morning long ago in the barn. He went to his library and fetched the little box that contained his special gift to his wife, a star of diamonds, not large, but dainty in design. He had written the card for it the day before. He tied the gift on the tree and then stood back. It was pretty, very pretty, and she would be surprised.

But he was not satisfied. He wanted to tell her . . . to tell her how much he loved her. It had been a long time since he had really told her, although he loved her in a very special way, much more than he ever had when they were young.

He had been fortunate that she had loved him . . . and how fortunate that he had been able to love! Ah, that was the true joy of life, the ability to love! For he was quite sure that some people were genuinely unable to love anyone. But love was alive in him, it still was.

It occurred to him suddenly that it was alive because long ago it had been born in him when he knew his father loved him. That was it: love alone could waken love.

And he could give the gift again and again. This morning, this blessed Christmas morning, he would give it to his beloved wife. He could write it down in a letter for her to read and keep forever. He went to his desk and began his love letter to his wife:

My Dearest Love. . . .

When it was finished he sealed it and tied it on the tree where she would see it the first thing when she came into the room. She would read it, surprised and then moved, and realize how very much he loved her.

He put out the light and went tiptoeing up the stairs. The star in the sky was gone, and the first rays of the sun were gleaming in the sky. Such a happy, happy Christmas!

Pearl S. Buck, *Colliers*, 12/23/55

Selfishness makes Christmas a burden: LOVE makes it a delight!

Norwegian Almond Rice Pudding

(Makes 8 to 10 servings)
2 cups water
2 tablespoons sugar
1/2 cup uncooked rice
1-1/2 tablespoons madeira or sherry
1 quart (4 cups) milk
1/2 cup heavy cream, whipped
1/8 teaspoon salt
1/4 cup slivered almonds
1 four-inch piece vanilla bean OR 1-1/2 teaspoons vanilla
1 whole almond per serving cup (optional)

METHOD: Heat water to boiling in medium-size sauce-pan, add rice, cook 5 minutes. Drain thoroughly. Heat milk to boiling with salt and vanilla bean (if using), in a medium-size saucepan. Stir in drained rice, lower heat. Simmer stirring con-stantly, for 5 minutes and cover. Cook, stirring occasionally for 45 minutes or until milk is almost absorbed and rice is tender and creamy. Stir in sugar, madeira, and vanilla (if you did not use vanilla bean). Chill.

Just before serving, remove vanilla bean. Whip cream, fold into pudding with slivered almonds. Serve in individual pudding cups (with a whole almond optional), garnished with cherry raspberry sauce.

CHERRY RASPBERRY SAUCE (makes 2 cups)
1 can (1 pound-1oz.) pitted dark sweet cherries
1 package (10 ozs.) frozen red raspberries in quick-thaw pouch, thawed
2 tablespoons sugar
4 teaspoons cornstarch

METHOD: Drain syrup from cherries and raspberries into a 2 cup measure. (You should have about 1-1/3 cups fruit juice.) Combine sugar and cornstarch in a medium-size saucepan, gradually stir in fruit juice. Cook, stirring constantly, over moderate heat until mixture thickens and just comes to boiling. Cool slightly and stir in fruit. SERVE warm or cooled, over Almond Rice Pudding! ENJOY!

(Ruth Strand-Lundeen)

The Inn That Missed Its Chance

(The landlord speaks, the time, A.D. 28)

What could be done? The inn was full of folks:
His Honor, Marcus Lucius, and his scribes
Who made the census; honorable men
From farthest Galilee, come hitherward
To be enrolled; high ladies and their lords;
The rich, the rabbis, such a noble throng
As Bethlehem had never seen before
And may not see again. And there they were,
Close-herded with their servants, till the inn
Was like a hive at swarming-time, and I
Was fairly crazed among them.

Could I know
That they were so impor-
tant? Just the two,
No servants, just a work-
man sort of man,
Leading a donkey, and his
wife thereon,

Drooping and pale . . . I saw them not myself.
My servants must have driven them away.
But had I seen them, how was I to know?
Were inns to welcome stragglers, up and down
In all our towns from Beersheba to Dan,
Till He should come? And how were men to know?
There was a sign, they say, a heavenly light
Resplendent; but I had no time for stars.
And there were songs of angels in the air
Out on the hills; but how was I to hear
Amid the thousand clamors of an inn?

Of course, if I had known them, who they were,
And who was He that should be born that night,
For now I learn that they will make Him King.

A second David, who will ransom us
From these Philistine Romans . . . who but He
That feeds an army with a loaf of bread,
And if a soldier falls, He touches him
And up he leaps, uninjured? Had I known,
I would have turned
The whole inn upside down,

His Honor, Marcus Lucius, and the rest,
And sent them all to stables.

So you have seen Him, stranger, and perhaps
Again may see Him? Prithee say for me
I did not know; and if He comes again,
As He surely will come, with retinue,
And banners, and an army . . . tell Him, my Lord,
That all my inn is His to make amends.

Alas, alas! to miss a chance like that!
This inn that might be chief among them all. . . .
The birthplace of the MESSIAH . . . had I known!

(Amos R. Wells)

How many observe Christ's birthday!
How few His precepts!
O! 'tis easier to keep holidays
than commandments.

(Benjamin Franklin)

Are you needing a colorful Christmas dessert? How about making the . . .

Norwegian Yifta

1 pound cranberries
1-1/2 to 2 cups salty soda cracker crumbs or graham cracker
1 cup sugar crumbs
1 cup water
1-1/2 to 2 cups whipping cream whipped and lightly sweetened
2 cups vanilla pudding

METHOD: Cook the cranberries with the water and sugar until the cranberries have burst. In a glass bowl or snifter, layer cranberry sauce, cracker crumbs, whipped cream, and pudding. It's pretty if last layer is whipped cream sprinkled with a few cracker crumbs. Refrigerate several hours or overnight. Serve chilled.

PS: "This is different enough so that you as the cook will have lots of questions to answer when you serve it. It is good!" adds Ruth.

(Ruth Strand-Lundeen)

93

It's All in Perspective

It was just a few days before Christmas. Two men who were next-door neighbors decided to go sailing while their wives went Christmas shopping. While the men were out in their sailboat, a storm caught them. The sea became angry and the men had great difficulty keeping the boat under control and afloat. As they maneuvered their way toward land, they hit a sandbar just beneath the ocean surface and the boat grounded. Both men jumped overboard and began to push and shove with all their strength, trying to get the boat into deeper water. With his feet knee-deep in mud and sand, the waves bouncing him against the side of the boat, his hair blowing wildly in the wind, and ocean spray in his face, one of the men said with a knowing grin: "It sure beats Christmas shopping . . . doesn't it?!"

One of a dad's larger dilemmas at Christmas is to convince his kids that he really is Santa Claus and his wife that he isn't.

Real Prayer

It was the Christmas season and a meeting was held in a small church for the announced purpose of praying for a local family that was having a tough time of it. The family was large and they didn't have enough food, or enough money to keep their home properly heated. As the people of the church prayed, there was some noise at the door of the church. They looked up and the young son of one of the elders had come in and shut the door with a bit of clumsiness and noise.

As all the people were staring at him he said, "My dad couldn't make it tonight to the prayer meeting so he sent his prayers in my wagon. Could you help me bring them in?"

His prayers consisted of a sack of potatoes, a quarter of beef, several bags of vegetables, flour, apples, and other assorted food staples. The prayer meeting was immediately adjourned!

Harold Kohn, *The Tinsel and the Hay*, adapted

Shakespeare and Christmas

Some say that ever 'gainst that season comes
Wherein our Saviour's birth is celebrated,
The bird of downing singeth all night long:
And then, they say, no spirit dare stir abroad;
The nights are wholesome; then no planets strike,
No fairy tales, nor witch hath power to charm,
So hallow'd and so gracious is the time.

(William Shakespeare)

It is a curious fact that this passage from "Hamlet" is the only one devoted to the topic of Christmas in all of the writings of Shakespeare. The great poet who dealt so completely with all the emotions of humanity for some reason was uninterested in that most joyous season of the year. He uses the word "Christmas" only three times in all the mass of his works, each time to describe a time of year only, not to talk about the day itself. The humorous writer Max Beerbohm offered an amusing reason for this omission. He asserted that Anne Hathaway, Shakespeare's wife, was born on Christmas Day. It is known that their marriage was not the happiest, as was evidenced by the famous bequest in Shakespeare's will leaving Anne Hathaway the "second-best" bed.

Whose Birthday?

Five-year-old Shaun was showing his Christmas presents to Grandma, when she asked, "Did you get everything you wanted for Christmas?"

Billy thought for a moment before he answered: "No, I didn't, Grandma. But that's okay. It wasn't my birthday."

Christmas shoppers can be described as the people with the brotherly shove.

It's really a stretch, a soul-stirring experience, to listen to Yuletide carolers standing in a typical Los Angeles smog singing, "It Came Upon a Midnight Clear"!

When you pay forty-five dollars for a Christmas tree (that was cut last July or August), you could say you've been trimmed more than the tree has.

Christmas is that time of the year when a whole lot of folks besides Santa find themselves in the red.

Christmas is that time of the year when parents spend more money on presents for the kids than they did on their honeymoon which started it all.

Nothing destroys the Christmas spirit faster than looking for a place to park.

Christmas shopping should always include purchasing toys for the kids that their father can have fun playing with.

Christmas shopping can be a race to see which gives out first . . . your feet or your patience or your money.

You can be sure that people who think that Christmas doesn't last all year don't have charge accounts.

Christmas holidays mean: Anticipation, preparation, perspiration, recreation, indigestion, frustration, prostration, and recuperation.

All in a Barn on a Winter Night

A baby slung in a feedbox
   Back in a barn, in a Bethlehem slum.
      A baby's first cry mixed with the crunch
         Of a mule's teeth on Bethlehem Christmas corn.
            Baby fists, softer than snowflakes in Norway.

The vagabond mother of Christ
   And the vagabond men of wisdom,
      All in a barn on a winter night,
         And a baby there in swaddling cloth on hay.
          WHY does the story never wear out?
            (Carl Sandburg)

Giving Something That Really Matters

We had a lovely director of Christian Education at our church in Virginia. Her name was Betty Jo Kendall. When Betty Jo came to our church, she organized a children's Christmas pageant. And she let the children decide what gifts they would give the Baby Jesus in the pageant. Some wanted to give Him stuffed animals, others wanted to give Him toys. One beautiful little child named Sallie Baldwin had several conversations with Betty Jo before she admitted what she wanted to give the Baby Jesus. Finally Betty Jo asked, "Sallie, what do you want to give Jesus?"

"Oh, I'm so embarrassed," said Sallie. "I shouldn't tell you."

"That's okay. What is it?"

"A kiss," she said.

And the night of the pageant, that is what she gave him. All the other angels brought their gifts of toys and animals. But Sallie bent over the manger and gave the little baby a kiss. A loving sigh went up from the congregation as we watched. She knew the secret of giving. The important thing at Christmas is to give something that matters. Something from the heart . . . because the heart is what Christmas is all about.

(Don Maddox, Corona, CA)

The Gift Exchange

It was the day after Christmas at a church in San Francisco. The pastor of the church was looking over the crèche when he noticed that the Baby Jesus was missing from among the figures. Immediately he turned and went outside and saw a little boy with a red wagon, and in the wagon was the figure of the little infant, Jesus.

So he walked up to the boy and asked, "Well, where did you get Him, my fine friend?"

The little boy replied, "I got Him from the church."

"And why did you take Him?"

The boy said, "Well, about a week before Christmas I prayed to the little Lord Jesus and I told Him if He would bring me a red wagon for Christmas I would give Him a ride around the block in it."

The Pastor's Story File, 12/88.